REDESIGN YOUR LIFE

Creating from Within

Elsa Mendoza

ISBN: 9798666236178

DEDICATION

To those who are seeking change, feeling stuck, and are unaware of their true power to create their reality—and to those who have no clue where and how to start redesigning their life...

INTRODUCTION

Sometimes it's difficult to be a human being. There is a lot to do, to feel, to understand, to remember, to take in, and to let go. It's an exhausting ride from when you were a kid to your adult life. There are days when you ask, "What is life? What is my purpose? Why am I here? How am I going to live the life I deserve? Do I have choices?"

You ask and look for answers. Sometimes advice from resources doesn't work, and maybe you cannot even relate to this advice, as your heart is closed to receiving it—and mostly because it does not include your beliefs, realizations, interpretations, and experiences. You realize you are following and taking advice based on the opinions of others, on their interpretations of their revelations. This worked for them, but won't work for you.

As you grow older, you learn that living your life is not about what people told you or what is described to you, but about your perspective and experience. Everyone has a choice to believe what will work and serve him or her.

I write to you neither as a life coach nor as someone who symbolically represents an organization. I do not have any attached titles or labels, but write to you as a fellow human, a fellow experiencer of the tides of life. I know we can relate with each other more this way. I desire neither to impose my teachings on you, nor to dictate or oblige you on what to do and what not to do.

I only desire to share pieces of my life experiences with the intention to inspire, uplift, motivate, encourage, and empower you. I am neither making grandiose claims that the wisdom and lessons in my life will work and serve you, nor am I persuading you that my truth will become your truth, too. Living with someone else's truth creates misalignment with who you are and damages yourself and your life. My truth is not yours, and yours is not mine.

I say all this because I believe every individual has his or her own interpretation and understanding. Everyone operates on a different level of awareness, and every event of life has a fresh revelation to each person who experiences it.

As you read, you may realize you already know or have come across a few topics discussed in this book. This usually happens when reading self-help books, as they are about human experiences, setbacks, and breakthroughs. Ask yourself these questions: "If I already know, have I ever heeded and followed my inner guidance, wisdom, and knowledge in my life? Is my life improving, or still the same? Do I feel stuck? Am I growing?"

If you think about it, the job of self-help books is to help you get motivated, inspired, encouraged, and empowered. The rest is up to you—the reader. Why? The only one responsible for living your life is YOU. No one can experience and live it for you. You cannot ask someone, "Hey, can you breathe for me for two hours?" or, "Hey, can you eat and drink for my body's sake?" or, "Hey, can you live my life, since I'm sick and tired of it?" No, you can't! You can't delegate that work, and you can't delegate the work of this book, either.

Motivation, encouragement, and empowerment are part of our essentials to live. There are abundant resources of these in life, but the best resource is the power within yourself. Yes, *you* have that power! It is the same power as the Infinite Source/Divine One/God. Within you is a wealth of wisdom. Through you, the energy of the Source flows. You are a spiritual being, from the same pure energy, incarnated from the non-physical, and a co-creator of the Infinite Creator. You are a part of God-consciousness. You are one with God...a god and goddess in human form.

Consider reading my third book, *Come Back To Love: Understandings and Reflections on Self-Love.* It outlines how, if you allow yourself to be open, you can have a better understanding of yourself and a deeper understanding of self-love. It challenges you to answer the question, "What are you doing to yourself?"

The book you are reading is the expanded version of a poem I wrote about life in my second book, *Wake Up Humanity: Poems About You and Me.* It is inviting you to answer the question, *"What are you doing with your life?"* I would like to share with you my observations, insights, wisdom, and lessons learned in life, hoping to inspire you to **redesign your life.**

While reading this book, you will encounter words such as God/Source/Energy/Infinite Creator/Divine Intelligence used interchangeably, as this book does not follow any specific beliefs. There will be questions at the end of each topic that can help you reflect on your life, in hopes of leading you to eventually answer the primary question of this book.

The primary intention of this book is to empower you—not because you are weak, but to help you remember your inherent power and activate it within yourself. The goal is to create and design a life worth living. I ask you only to have an open heart and mind while reading this book. You are welcome to apply any wisdom and lesson that resonated with you.

Peace, joy, and love,

Elsa Mendoza, CCC
Long Beach, CA

A desire calls for a creation and change
To change, one must open
To open, one must allow
To allow, one must surrender
To surrender, one must accept
To accept, one must heal
To heal, one must change oneself first
To change oneself, one must go within
To go within, one must self-inquire
To self-inquire, one must observe
To observe, one must quiet the mind
To quiet the mind, one must be still
To be still, one must be aware
To be aware, one must be alive
To be alive, one must live
To live is to experience life

Elsa Mendoza

CONTENTS

DEDICATION **iii**

INTRODUCTION **v**

CHAPTER ONE: LIFE'S BIG QUESTIONS **1**

WHAT IS LIFE? 1

WHAT IS MY PURPOSE? 13

WHY AM I HERE? 19

CHAPTER TWO: CREATING FROM WITHIN **23**

UNDERSTANDING THE BASICS OF THE LAW OF ATTRACTION 26

THE CREATION PROCESS 27

CHAPTER THREE: REDESIGNING YOUR LIFE **47**

KEYS *48*

REMINDERS *51*

CHAPTER FOUR: DESIGN REFERENCES **57**

THE NONPHYSICAL GUIDES 58

CHAPTER FIVE: THE BEAUTIFUL LIFE **71**

COMMON OBSTACLES 72

THE EXPERIENCE 73

OPPORTUNITIES 86

AUTHOR'S NOTE **99**

REQUEST **105**

ACKNOWLEDGEMENTS **107**

ABOUT THE AUTHOR **109**

ALSO BY ELSA MENDOZA **111**

CONNECT WITH THE AUTHOR **113**

REFERENCES **115**

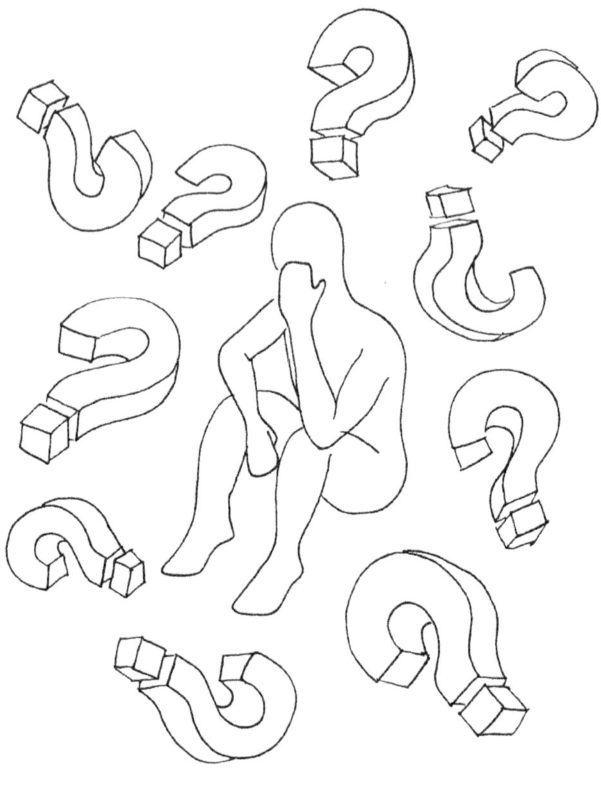

CHAPTER ONE

LIFE'S BIG QUESTIONS

WHAT IS LIFE?

One morning in 2008, all ready to go to work, I suddenly felt weak and exhausted. I lay on my bed and thought to myself, *the day hasn't started yet, but I am already fatigued.* After gaining my strength, I drove to work. I turned off the radio, as I could not stand any sound, not even my favorite songs. At work, I had a hard time balancing myself in my chair, as if a force was pulling me down. I remembered the same uncomfortable feeling I had a few months back, during which I noticed inexplicable bruising on my body. I just ignored it.

Then, around three in the afternoon, I started gasping for breath. My concerned and panicked co-workers came to my side; one got on the phone to call 911, and another hurriedly ran to get our manager. The entourage of ambulances and fire trucks soon came. Paramedics picked me up and transported me to the nearby hospital. I was so anxious I started crying.

In the hospital, I was told that I passed out after giving my urine sample. I remembered putting my underwear back on and standing before the sink, washing my hands. Then everything went blank.

The next thing I remembered was walking in slow motion along the hallway of my apartment, trying to reach my bedroom where a bright light awaited. As I got closer, it became brighter, and it mesmerized me. I felt so much love in the presence of the bright light, a pure, non-judgmental, no-expectation kind of love...a love I hadn't physically experienced before. I wanted to stay there forever.

Then I heard someone call my name. I opened my eyes, confused that I was lying on the ground and surrounded by people wearing navy blue scrubs. I smelled my saliva frothing in my mouth—I later learned that happened when I was convulsing while unconscious. I felt a pressure on my left wrist and heard a woman's voice shout, "She's got a pulse!" Someone scooped me up from the floor, put me on a stretcher, and they wheeled me to the emergency area.

The doctors diagnosed me with Aplastic Anemia. After blood transfusions, blood tests, self-injections to increase white blood cells, a painful bone marrow aspiration, and a complete change in diet, I got well and fully recovered after three years and eight months. It was a long journey and the start of a series of changes in lifestyle, relationships with others, and relationship with myself.

After I healed from this health ordeal, I had an epiphany. I awoke from a deep slumber. It was a reboot...a rebirth. I became conscious in a deeper sense. I got curious, and I questioned everything. "Now what? What's next? What is the message of all this? What is happening? What am I doing in this world?" It was as if I was living life for the first time and feeling everything for the first time. I was hungry for answers about the existence of everything, especially about the truth of the world, humanity, God—and most of all, myself and my life.

Life has changed since then. I sought answers to fill in my curiosity. I learned to meditate. I immersed myself in reading books and watching documentaries about spirituality. I listened to spiritual teachers. I opened and allowed myself to process the messages, inspiration, and wisdom I received. Then, I applied only those that worked for me and disregarded old beliefs. I unlearned and I learned. I still do.

I started noticing the clarity of the path I am walking on, the essence of my journey, and the beauty of life. My victim mindset—born from my experiences of being beaten up and feeling unloved by parents, especially my father—was one that I held onto from age five until my early twenties. I learned to transform my mindset from being a victim to being an inspired, creative being. I realized that all this happened to my benefit. My mindset shaped me and changed my perspectives and my attitude. I love what I have become and who I am becoming now. It fulfills joy in the journey.

It is always during challenging times that a person seeks to find what they are looking for—the answers, the clarity, and the experiences they desire. But until then, there will be days where you just don't know how to continue living your life. Some days you'd ask, "When does it end?" Sometimes you feel alive, and sometimes you feel down.

There are days when even the most minuscule things contribute to your concerns. You can't decide what to eat, drink, cook, or order to-go. You even contemplate whether or not to put makeup on or shave. Sometimes it is even hard to decide what to wear for work, or if you should even go to work—yes, it's a routine! Even if you have a set schedule, you still ask these questions. *Ugh, what a mundane life,* you say to yourself. Why do we keep repeating this cycle?

There are days, too, where you pause and think of other people, your beloved pet and other animals. Even little critters go through the same daily cycle as yours, only without your exact to-dos. You wonder, *Do they ask the same questions as I do? How do they live? How do they survive life, every single day?* Then you ask again, *Why do I experience these? Why do I have questions? What is life, anyway?*

Perhaps, such is life, you think with a sigh...then a change in your situation happens and you realize it's not dull all the time. Can life be constant and erratic? Is a day consistent with the rise of the sun until it sets, the air that you breathe, the sound of noise and message of silence, the rain that dances? The day always comes and shows up for you. *It must be constant*, you declare.

Yes, what is life all about? What is it exactly? Where and how did it start? Does it end? Who created it? There are a lot of interesting ideas about how life started. People have come up with theories and are still trying their best to get the answers, scientifically and philosophically.

Blaise Pascal, a French scientist and mathematician in the seventeenth century, said in his book, *Pensees*, "When I consider the short duration of my life, swallowed up in an eternity before and after, the little space I fill engulfed in the infinite immensity of spaces whereof I know nothing, and which know nothing of me, I am terrified. The eternal silence of these infinite spaces frightens me."

Despite mysteries of its origin, I think some of us can agree that there is a *consciousness* we are all a part of, and a *force* or *energy* that has existed even before we could identify that it is life itself. This force is something constant that holds everything, including us, together from nothing. This nothingness and formlessness is the Source of all. Many call this God, Infinite Creator, Supreme Being, Divine Intelligence, Energy, or Pure Consciousness. Regardless of what one calls it, I believe these terms are the same with life, where you and I are the active partakers, witnesses, and experiencers.

I suppose no one can fathom Divine Intelligence. To understand Divine Intelligence, one must be out of one's intelligence. To understand the Infinite Creator, one must be out of one's mind. It is a mind-boggling, immeasurable mystery.

Life is working for everyone's benefit, but not everyone sees, feels, agrees, believes, or cares about it. We all have that knowledge on how to live our lives. We also yearn to live it peacefully, easily, beautifully, and happily. We have interpreted and accepted this knowledge as to result more in surviving and existing than fully living. We cannot escape having experiences of pain and suffering, so we sometimes numb ourselves just to keep going. We sometimes feel that we're going somewhere but getting nowhere, going in circles, cycles, rhythms. We enter a mundane routine.

Could life be a series of tests? What causes its fluctuations? What are the lessons from these experiences? How is this happening? We are in a physical world of the relative, of polarity, where choices and opposites are extant and experienced. This means that there will be endless cycles and situations where we can witness the ebb and flow of life. But one thing is for sure: ***contrast is vital to help us identify what we want and do not want.***

Pain and suffering must be experienced to know joy and bliss. Contrast is present to distinguish between negative and positive, chaos and harmony, sour and sweet, black and white. I had to be ill to experience healing; I had to hate myself and be alone to experience self-love; and I had to be weak and in my lowest moments to experience and activate my power again to live the life I desired.

Could life have a purpose? I realized that life causes us to *remember who we are and who we are not* through the continuous creation of our reality, as well as our experiences of success and failure. Through the remembrance of our nature, we ***rediscover our power***. We get back up and thrive in our difficulties. We realize that in our lowest moments, we find our true powerful selves, too.

Try recalling your painful memories and notice where you are at this present moment. There might be a lot of tears shed and vulnerability, but here you are now, smiling or probably laughing about it, right? You have moved on, and you are now a tougher and stronger you, ready to rewrite a fresh story of your life, complete with your realizations, wisdom, and lessons learned. Life is then about *creation,* and the materialization of our ideas and passions to our purpose.

I realize that *the purpose of life is for us to give it purpose, add meaning to it, and experience fully living it.*

It is a significant and a constant reminder of our connection and oneness with the Divine Intelligence/ Divine Consciousness through co-creating.

It is *an incessant cycle of remembrance of our true non-physical nature.* It is being realized in our conscious and unconscious decisions, actions, efforts, and creations, leading to the evolution of our souls.

It is more about us as *creators* than the dramas and problems that we have created and got stuck with. **It is also where we experience our essence through our relationships as physical beings...as humans.**

When I look back through my memories and try to put meaning to them, I observe my realization in the present, as the present moment is the only time I believe exists. Everything is happening in the moment of *now*.

When you plan for the future, the planning takes place in the present. Even when you try to relive your past and talk about it, the conversation is in the present, isn't it? I'm writing about this now, discussing the past and future with you. Therefore, *life is now,* not yesterday and not tomorrow. Where are you?

You may now stop worrying about the future, as it always comes in the present moment. We cannot predict the future, but we can create the future by how we're acting and what we're doing now.

Some have taken life so seriously that they have caused themselves illnesses or to miss the joy life brings. I am not saying to take life as a joke. I am only referring to living life with ease.

Some could not live the life that they would like to have, for they are afraid to be who they truly want to be. Therefore, they live within the expectation, dictation, and approval of others to feel safe and have a sense of belongingness.

In the past, I feared being judged by people and by God because of my relationship and religious preferences. My fears and limiting beliefs crippled me. The epiphany I had after my near-death experience—that there's only love—helped me release myself from these fears and limitations.

We can then consider life as *freedom*. We all have a choice and can decide how we would like to live our lives. We decide who, what, how, and where we would like to be and to go, what to believe in, and whether to enjoy life or be miserable every moment. And so, **life is not a test where you are subject to fail or to pass, but it is full of invitations and opportunities to create a better life: your preferred life.**

The sprouting of plants, budding of fruits, blooming of flowers, a caterpillar transforming to a butterfly, a human conceiving a child—life is about *process and growth*. We no longer speak, act, think, reason, understand, and live like we did when we were five years old or in our teens, right? Observe where you are now and compare where you were before. You have grown and are still growing, physically, mentally, emotionally, and spiritually. You have changed and are still changing.

Nothing and nobody truly remains unchanged, as *change* is the only permanent thing. This change can help us understand and manage our expectations from people, as they have also changed and keep on changing.

The breeze of the wind, the rushing sound of the rivers and oceans, chirps of birds, cries of puppies, the touch of a loved one. Life is about *experiences,* about satisfying our senses. One cannot deny the beauty of life in the physical. You and I are witnesses of this life, as are all other sentient beings.

As conscious beings, we witness life through our *inward and outward experiences.* We derive these experiences from our projections and perceptions. Projection is seeing life from our inner beliefs, and perception is our outside awareness.

We see the world as we are, the people as we are, situations as we are, and God as we are. If you observe life, it can be meaningful or meaningless. It can be nothing or something, full or empty. **It all depends on one's perspective, on how one views the world in his lens. Life is dependent on one's interpretation of the revelations it brings.**

Life is a dance to its music, tempo, and flow. Every being that experiences it interprets life in unique ways—making an individualized journey. It's on our own accord to seize and live it. How life is unfolding in front of you is how you are *becoming* from within, as you are the director, writer, editor, and actor of your story. You are the creator of your experience, your world, and your reality.

You are a part of an entire consciousness, the pure God-consciousness. You may have thought you are separate from Divinity, but know that nothing can ever separate you from God, as you are the embodiment and the physical extension of the Source. The Universe is YOU! Its components are in you, the same energy, atoms, and elements, and this is already a proven fact by scientists. Life is **US**.

To summarize, life is a synonym of love and God. The active participants are you, me, and all other sentient beings. Life is *us*. It constantly reminds us that we are in partnership with the Infinite Creator throughout our experience of it. It is a process, an endless cycle of learning, healing, renewing, and discovering our powers as creators. It is about remembering our genuine nature from our experiences brought by our freedom of choice. It is also about growth, from the manifestation of our creation leading to the evolution of our souls and the expansion of the Universe. Life exists only in the present moment.

REFLECTIONS

What is the meaning of life for you?

How do you see life based on your experiences

What have you realized about life?

WHAT IS MY PURPOSE?

In life, so many are still at a loss when it comes to finding their purpose. Among the top careers people want to be include: a doctor, a police officer, a journalist, a politician, a lawyer, and a scientist. Some achieve these goals. Others get stuck in limbo, floating like a balloon going nowhere. The rest are still figuring it out.

Is our true purpose to be a doctor or a police officer? What really is our purpose?

Our sole purpose is to *create.*

Create what? You are creating the **environment you would like to be in and the life you would like to have through the experiences of who you have become and are becoming. This leads to your specific purpose.**

Who you are, what you have, and where you are at present constitute your creations. It is not limited, confined, or permanent, as it is about the *joyful expansion* through one's endless creation.

Perhaps you could not find your specific purpose because it is motivated by doing and getting, not by being and letting. What do I mean? You have focused your purpose on the *result* rather than knowing your *inner* purpose first.

What is my inner purpose, then? **It is being in alignment with the truth of who you are. Who you are is about peace, joy, abundance, and love**.

Achieving your specific purpose requires focus on your **becomingness. In other words, you must focus on who you are becoming during the creation process of your life experiences.** Sometimes you lose your focus, and so you end up in an endless search of what to do and who to be. You end up copying what others do, and that sometimes results in countless failures.

You can realize your *specific purpose* by identifying the **reason behind your reason, the why behind your why, and the sponsoring thought of your thought**.

Here are some ways I figured out my specific purpose that you may find helpful:

Years ago, I included "publishing a book" in my bucket list. Then it sat there for two years. I didn't know what my purpose was at first, as it was only a desire. A desire is a call for creation and change. I had no clue how to publish a book until I became a life coach.

In life-coaching sessions with clients, I realized I could coach and help more people by sharing my life story, realizations, and wisdom. I became a life coach first before becoming an author, but becoming a life coach and listening to my own advice eventually led to me publishing books.

My reasons are to inspire, uplift, encourage, and empower. Having these reasons, I became much clearer with my intention, which differs slightly from my purpose.

To summarize my experience:

1. **My sponsoring thought behind my thought** was the desire that I kept thinking about, which was to self-publish a book and share my story.
2. **My becomingness** was the processes, realizations, and experiences I went through in becoming a life coach first. It included how I was becoming *within* before achieving my specific purpose.
3. **My intention** was to publish inspirational books for upliftment, encouragement, and empowerment.
4. **My specific purpose, or the "why behind my why"** was to help and coach more people through my books.
5. **My inner purpose was** to be in alignment with the truth of who I am, which was and is about peace, joy, and love. My creations were on these truths.

Helpful questions to figure out your inner purpose:

1. Who am I?
2. Who am I not?
3. What is my role?
4. What am I about?

5. Why am I here?
6. What is my truth?
7. Am I living my truth?

Helpful questions to figure out your specific purpose:

1. What do I really want?
2. Why do I want it?
3. How am I going to get to what I want?
4. What would I like to do with what I want?
5. Who do I want to become from what I want?
6. How will this desire serve me?
7. What would I like to offer from what I want?
8. Is this in alignment with my truth?

Your inner purpose is **to be in alignment with the truth of who you are, which is about peace, joy, abundance, and love.** May these truths inspire your creations.

Your sole purpose is to create experiences leading to your *specific purpose.* It is unique to you and *what you offer to the world.*

Your *intention* is your *direction, execution* and *how you can make your specific purpose happen in the creation process.*

You can let your specific purpose sit and mature. Contemplate first, before jumping onto something immediately without an absolute clarity. See how and who you are becoming in your beingness. Align with your truth. Ruminate on it more.

You do not have to go somewhere to find your specific purpose. No one is in a hurry, except your thoughts and the stressful stories you add to them. You do not have to look anywhere for your path, as *where you are now is somewhere on the path you're supposed to be on...look within yourself.* Start wherever you are at this moment and see how it unfolds for you!

REFLECTIONS

What is your purpose?

Are you in alignment with the truth of who you are?

Have you figured out your specific purpose? How?

What is your specific purpose? How are you going to achieve your specific purpose then?

What is your intention?

WHY AM I HERE?

Since life is constant and can have its tides only by the meaning you put into it, then you are *to live the meaning as you have defined it.*

There are reasons you exist in this physical world:

1. You are here to live your purpose. Your purpose is to *create* and to be in alignment with your truth, as well as to offer what you created to the world.

2. You are here to know that you are a creator and the created, the observer and the observed, the experiencer and the experienced, an attractor, doer, thinker, realizer, inviter, allower, and receiver. You are here to experience the real essence of YOU.

3. You are here to do what you were born with. Experience your passion with your innate talents. It is *what you love to do.* It is where your heart sings, your eyes sparkle, your feet dance. It is where you excel.

4. You are here *to be yourself.* You ought to be what you create of yourself in the creation process. You could be happy, sad, generous, selfish, successful, or not. You should experience who and what you are becoming.

5. You are here to become the grandest version of you. You are here to love, through the

experiences and environment you have created for yourself.

6. You are here to remember your true natural states: peace, joy, and love. You are here to be propelled by and in the world of contrast. This contrast helps you know your wanted and unwanted preferences. It involves thriving from challenges in situations and relationships to achieve your purpose.
7. You are here to evolve, teach, remind, inspire, bring light to, and share with others the wisdom learned from your creation journeys or epiphanies.
8. You are here to experience your power within and perform miracles that may remind others of their own power.
9. You are here to co-create and experience your oneness with the other sentient beings and with Infinite Creator/God through the creation process.
10. You are here *to be happy and to enjoy a beautiful life.*

REFLECTIONS

Why are you here?

How are you living your reasons for being here? What are your choices?

Are you focused on who and what you are becoming? Who, what and how are you becoming?

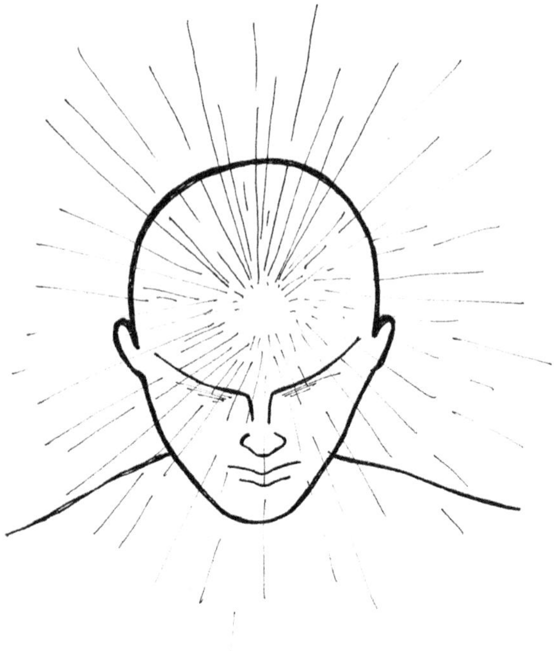

CHAPTER TWO

CREATING FROM WITHIN

Creating from within is about the utilization of the power inside of you. It is using your spiritual mind and activating it accurately to serve yourself and everyone else. It is using the innate wisdom from Divine Intelligence for your joyful expansion.

If there's one thing I was certain of during my health ordeal in 2008 that kept me confident and calm—even feeling indestructible, despite the different prognosis of the doctors (leukemia, lupus) and their proposal for a bone marrow transplant—it was my faith.

Through the eyes of the many, I was sick, but I looked at my situation as just stress manifesting in the physical—in my body. "I'm just stressed out; what are you talking about?" These were my usual thoughts whenever a doctor would visit me in my hospital bed.

I had so much faith and confidence that I challenged my doctors to give me reasons I needed to go through the proposed transplant. In the end, I didn't have to do the transplant. I still submitted to my doctor's orders and the routine check-ups, as I believed they were there because they were the cooperative elements of my healing journey. I trusted the process.

My faith kept me whole inside. I felt like nobody and nothing could harm, damage, or destroy me, especially not the illness I had. This faith reminded me of my connection, oneness, and partnership with the Infinite Creator/Divine Intelligence. It gave me clarity that helped me see through life and allowed me to do things I previously deemed impossible. It helped me remember who I am and what I am capable of.

This faith also brought me to understand my capabilities and acknowledge my role in why some things and situations that I wanted to happen, happened, and why others did not come to fruition.

I didn't realize that the four months of being on sick leave were the start of a wonderful journey that would transform my life. This journey was the answer to the questions after my near-death experience. It led me to search and study for many hours about spirituality, even taking a quick course to understand metaphysics. One day I chanced upon the Oprah show where they were discussing the Law of Attraction. I watched and listened intently, then quickly purchased the book *The Secret*. I allowed myself to receive the wisdom and applied it to my life, which opened my eyes to many more resources of the Law of Attraction (LOA).

While on sick leave, I had a lot of time to heal so I could get back to work. How did I get well? My understanding of the principles and practice of the Law of Attraction helped me a lot, not only with my healing but also in dealing with my daily life from 2008 to the present. Little did I know that I had already experienced the workings of this law in my life. You might have, too.

According to many scholars and followers of LOA, it has always existed and has been active since the world began. However, it was first mentioned only in the year 1877 by author Helena Blavatsky, followed by the articulation of another author, Prentice Mulford, in 1886.

As everyone has a unique way of processing and interpreting information, everyone has a different awareness of things. That said, you have the choice to believe (or not) the information I will share with you. You are welcome to search about this law further. But for the meantime, have an open mind with what you're about to read. I also know that words are not effective teachers—experience is. As an author, I base the words in all my books on my experiences expressed and shared to the masses for inspiration. I do this as an invitation to experience, as an upliftment, as a reminder, as encouragement, and as empowerment.

Understanding the Basics of the Law of Attraction:

What is it and how does it work?

The LOA describes the positive and negative thoughts we think about and brings them to a physical manifestation of our reality. Like energy attracts like energy. It acts like a manager of many of our vibrations.

To remember in the process of creation:

- **Universe** – a magnetic field of energies. Other names include God/Source.
- **You** – a vibrational, creative, pure, energy-emitting being with the same composition as the Universe. You are a spiritual, non-physical, and physical being, a creator, thinker, attractor, receiver, allower, inviter, experiencer, and observer.
- **Thoughts, words, deeds** – tools of creation. They are energies.
- **Desire** – idea/thought/a call for creation to physical manifestation.
- **Contrast** – this is in our physical world. It asks one to identify wanted and unwanted preferences.
- **Beliefs** – positive and negative thoughts that we constantly think about.

- **Vibration** – energy we emit and broadcast, interpreted by our emotions.
- **Alignment** – our vibrations, thoughts, and emotions that are attuned and matched with our desires.

The Creation Process:

As mentioned in Chapter One, to understand the Divine Intelligence, one must be out of one's intelligence, and to understand the Infinite Creator, one must be out of one's mind. It is a mind-boggling, immeasurable mystery. Explaining the laws of the Universe has quite the same effect on our scientists, as presented by their observations and theories.

According to the European Space Agency, the Universe is thought to comprise three types of substance: normal matter, "dark matter," and "dark energy." Normal matter comprises the atoms that make up stars, planets, **human beings,** and every other visible object in the Universe.

As our composition is the same as the Universe's, we can say we have massive amounts of energy locked up in molecules, composed of several atoms in high-speed vibration in our human body. We can compare the Universe to a field of consciousness—a magnetic field of energies and vibrations. The Universe is us.

Our consciousness is a mixture of perceptions, sensations, thoughts, and emotions. **Thoughts, words, and actions** are the tools of creation. They are energies attracting like energies, through the Law of Attraction. We are energy beings, emitting frequencies through our chosen thoughts as the focus of our attention.

Emotions are energies in motion and are indicators of whether we are thinking thoughts that are or are not in alignment with what we desire. They help us direct our thoughts, too.

We are in an environment where everything is in motion. Everything vibrates. This law is about energy attracting like energy and your vibration matching the same vibration. It is mirroring back to us whatever energy or vibration we give out and **works effectively when we are in the same vibration of whatever we desire.**

We were pure energy and vibrational beings before we became humans in this physical world or the world of contrast. We vibrate or emit frequencies and, as humans, these frequencies tell us the state we're in through what and who we have attracted in our lives.

In the creation process, one must know one's role. As discussed in the previous topic, your sole purpose is to create, which then makes you a *creator*. You are also the thinker, attractor, inviter, allower, receiver, experiencer, and an observer. You are both a non-physical and a physical being. You live in this physical world where it is also the world of polarity, relativity, and contrast. They are important in the creation process.

Your game is *creation*, which is the eternal game of this Universe. As a creator, you never stop creating. Nothing is completed because desires will keep multiplying. Changes will keep appearing. You are a game changer. You keep evolving. You only become a master of being a deliberate creator.

What is a deliberate creator? A deliberate creator is a conscious creator. He understands his power through the tools of creation and its effects on himself and others. He knows his ability to focus and easily align with his desires. He believes that his desires result from what is expected for him to receive, and that everything is already done even before he witnesses it in the physical. He acts and lives as if it's already happening.

The game of creation also means contrast is present. It is a contributor to your physical growth and evolution, prompting you to ask and have clarity until the achievement of your desires. Contrast helps you identify what you want and do not want, leading you to your spiritual growth, too.

Physical growth can pertain to having a healthy body that can work and serve you for many years without illnesses. It can also refer to having all your material desires. They manifested from taking care of your body, and the stuff that you take in like food, exposure to influences, and sources.

Spiritual growth is about being aware, more in touch with your divine self, more aligned with the truth of who you are, more tuned in to love, and more open to embracing your true essence and power. This growth takes place amid your emotional challenges, changes in life, decisions you make, and conflicts in relationships with people and especially with yourself.

Desire is where the creation process starts. It is where ideas are born. It is the soul wanting to experience itself through you for expansion and evolution. For this desire to come to physical manifestation, it requires **the focus of your attention, as well as believing in and allowing your satisfaction through your emotions**. How does one focus? Through thinking of the same thoughts in alignment with your desires, what you want to experience, and a positive outcome shown by your positive emotions.

In my personal experience, the manifestation through the practice of LOA was in the healing of my illness. My healing manifested through constant thoughts of good health. I visualized and allowed myself to focus more on the result of being healthy, thinking good thoughts that gave me satisfaction. The Universe then brought it to its full fruition, as my thoughts, beliefs, feelings, and expectations were in *alignment* with what I wanted: good health.

My experiences show that creation manifested through **habitual thinking**. **Our beliefs are just the repetitive thoughts that we keep thinking about.** If you dig deeper, everything originated from the non-physical world, if you will, and it's always working with us. It makes sense. We cannot see thoughts, emotions, and vibrations, right?

LOA's secret: The actual work is in *alignment*.

Repetition works in impressing upon your subconscious with words of life and positivity. As the subconscious mind is non-judgmental, it takes in whatever the conscious mind commands. You can then consider being cautious of what you feed it—of your self-talk.

Learn more about the subconscious mind, non-physical world, and quantum physics by exposing yourself to the works of Joseph Murphy, Deepak Chopra, and Craig Jackson.

The belief you keep thinking about mixed with your strong emotions manifests fast to the physical. Your world, type of environment, people you surround yourself with, and situations you engage yourself with are those you have attracted and manifested through your focus of attention or through the thoughts you have chosen and consumed.

Every single moment you are in the process of creation. Observe your thought process, your self-talk, and the quality of your life daily. If your constant thought quality is positive, then you can attract and experience more positivity, as your vibration is positive. It works exactly the same way with negativity.

Old thoughts that you may have already forgotten, but may have focused on in the past, can manifest in the present. This is how active LOA is.

As the observer and experiencer of what is, you also have the power to choose your experience by changing your thought quality. You cannot expect a positive outcome and declare or say positive words while you feel negative. With the thousands of thoughts you have daily, you can monitor them easily by **paying attention to how you feel**.

Let's say you do not like where you are, and want to change your way of thinking. How do you change the way you think? **By choosing and dwelling on good, positive thoughts, you manifest enjoyable experiences, therefore changing your vibration.**

Again, **feelings and emotions are guides. They are the indicators of the quality of the thoughts you think about.** Negative emotions arise from dwelling on thoughts not in alignment with your desires or with what you want. It's a disadvantage to you if you keep dwelling on these. Think about it. The best examples for this are the painful memories and regrets in the past you keep replaying in your mind, which is why your current feelings and situations are still about pain and regret. More of these emotions show up in your life as you dwell on them. It's time to leave pain and have a celebration. Shift your consciousness to experience the manifestations of your genuine desires.

Negative emotions can also serve as a warning for you to go back to thinking positive thoughts so you may feel good again. You may start with thinking thoughts that offer relief to you. It is all about choosing and saying statements derived from better thoughts that contribute to your feeling relieved. This is how you go back to being and feeling positive and in alignment with your desires. It takes practice, but soon you will master them and see the endless manifestations of what you want.

Examples:

1. **Negative thoughts/self-talks/stressful statements:** *"I am sick and tired of having no money. Money is hard. Money doesn't grow on trees. I have to work hard."*

   A shift to positive/better thoughts/self-talks/ relieving statements: *"I have a job. I got this job easily. I also have other job options and opportunities. I can get enjoyable, paying jobs. Money is everywhere, not only in jobs. I am skillful and talented."*

2. **Negative thoughts/self-talks/stressful statements: "***I am tired of being sad. I am tired of having pain. I don't want to suffer anymore. I want to be happy."*

   A shift to positive/better thoughts/self-talks/ relieving statements: *"Everyone gets sad. It's normal to feel this way sometimes. I honor my feelings. I can get over it. It's not painful all the* *time. I don't suffer the whole day anyway. I always thrive. I have choices. I can be happy again."*

3. **Negative thoughts/self-talks/stressful state ments:** *"I hate how I look. I feel fat and ugly. I don't like how the way I dress up. I feel worthless."*

   A shift to positive/better thoughts/self-talks/ relieving statements: "*I am unique. I can accept how I look like. I can learn to dress up nicely. I can choose a healthier lifestyle. I am at peace with my choices. I can appreciate myself for what I am. I can love myself for who I am."*

Nothing manifests if there isn't a belief that it will. The Universe listens to how you *feel*. It matches the vibration you're emitting. When you better your focus or fix your thinking, life fixes itself, you feel good all the time, see more opportunities and advantages, and you appreciate where you are.

As explained previously, life is about growth. *Evolution* is the catalyst of creation. We are creators and also the created, determined by our experiences. We are co-creators of the Infinite Creator.

As we create our realities and anew ourselves based on our desires—and the ideas of ourselves on how and who we would like to be—we begin to live the truth of what we intuitively know about ourselves. We experience the god within us.

When I say "the god within us," I'm referring to us as divine, spiritual beings with unlimited powers within us. These include the power to heal despite our capacity to harm, to live in peace despite all the chaos, to be confident of abundance despite poverty, to see harmony despite disorder, to offer unconditional love to everyone no matter what, to thrive from challenges, and to manage emotions and thoughts with the same wisdom flowing through you as does the Source/God.

This refers to an integrated life as a non-physical and physical being in the physical world. Remember, you originated from pure consciousness; you are energy from nothingness.

This is for you to realize the powers within you and share them with others, that it may remind them of the same powers and activate them in their lives, too. We are miracles, the embodiment of life and love, the same love of a living God that flows through us. Some call this **higher self, consciousness, soul, spirit, and inner being.**

Human beings/masters/gods like Jesus and Buddha walked on this earth and understood being deliberate creators. They showed the possibilities, wonders, and miracles of the human powers and how they can be used to create a beautiful life. May they inspire us to emulate, through our **thoughts, words, and actions,** a powerful faith in the Universe. They fully understood the power of thoughts and how they work, and they live in alignment with them. Let's ponder on their sayings.

The Sayings of Buddha:

> *"Every human being is the author of his own health or disease."*
>
> *"We are shaped by our thoughts; we become what we think. When the mind is pure, joy follows like a shadow that never leaves."*
>
> *"All that we are is the result of what we have thought. If a man speaks or acts with an evil thought, pain follows him. If a man speaks or acts with a pure thought, happiness follows him, like a shadow that never leaves him."*
>
> *"What we are today comes from our thoughts of yesterday, and our present thoughts build our life of tomorrow: Our life is the creation of our mind."*
>
> *"Your worst enemy cannot harm you as much as your own thoughts, unguarded. But once mastered, no one can help you as much."*

The Sayings of Jesus:

> *"Jesus said to him, 'If you can believe, all things are possible to them that believe.'" (Mark 9:23)*

> *"For God gave us a spirit not of fear but of power and love and self-control." (2 Timothy 1:7)*
>
> *"And whatever you ask in prayer, you will receive, if you have faith." (Matthew 21:22)*
>
> *"You will also decree a thing, and it will be established for you." (Job 22:28)*
>
> *"For as a man thinks in his heart, so is he." (Proverbs 23:7)*

Everything that you see in this physical world is the manifestation of people's ideas. These ideas are thoughts that originated from desires.

Once I understood and discovered our inherent powers, I no longer looked at myself the same way. I realized I am not just a physical body made of skin, bones, and muscles. I am not a victim of circumstances, helpless and dependent on someone else's approval. NO! We have focused so much on our physicality that we have forgotten the non-physical parts of us. We are spiritual beings going through the human experience.

I can only strongly encourage you to stop being afraid to discover and **own your power**—and, perhaps, to admit that you alone are the one who attracted and are responsible for what has happened and what is happening in your life.

Acknowledging you are responsible does not mean you need to start blaming yourself for your current life situation, but it does mean you need to realize that you can create as many experiences as you want that serve you, so you can be who and how you want to be. This realization brings you more clarity of your power.

You are in control, just as the Divine Intelligence/God is, as you are the embodiment of the Divine, the physical extension of the Source. You are a child of God made from God's image and likeness. This image and likeness refers to your abilities and power. Being in control means **you are recognizing, believing, and using the gift of freewill and acknowledging your oneness to create miracles with the Divine.**

You are a co-creator of the Infinite Creator. You cannot be separate from It/Him/Her/Them. How could you be? Understand that everything and everywhere is of God. One can only separate himself because of his chosen beliefs influenced and created by men, based on the fearful ego's belief system and not on the Divine Intelligence's system. There is only one source, one consciousness—though there are many unique interpretations. We are such powerful, vibrational, creative beings.

Understand your power and the Law of Attraction further by exposing yourself to the works of Abraham Hicks, Andrea Schulman, Helena Bravatsky, Prentice Mulford, Wallace D. Wattles, and Justin Perry.

LOA ILLUSTRATION

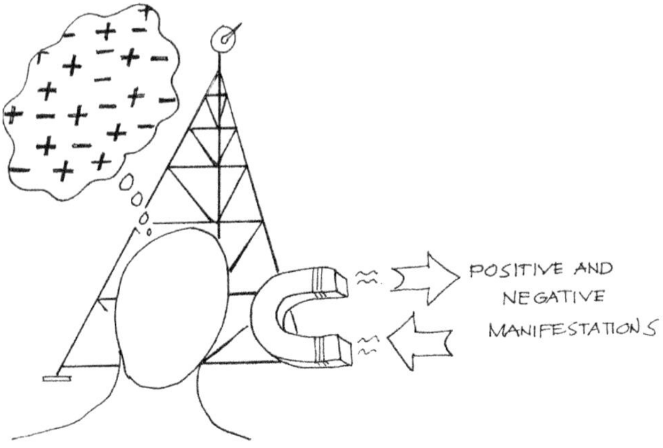

Tips to Make LOA Work and Serve You Well:

- Believe/Trust/Faith
- Think and choose positive thoughts
- Focus only on what you want and align with it
- Feel good as much as you can
- Speak life
- Act as if your desires are already happening—this is alignment
- Be aware of and be guided by your emotions as indicators of the quality of thoughts you're thinking
- Expose and surround yourself more with positive energy and sources

Benefits and Effects of Law of Attraction:

- You understand the game of the Universe
- You realize the abundance of resources available for you
- Everything is possible to be, do, and have
- You can change your circumstances
- You have freedom to create
- You notice your power within

- You think better thoughts
- You understand and manage your emotions better
- You become more appreciative of life
- You become present-moment-oriented
- You become happier
- You become healthier
- You become more loving
- You become more generous

Reasons LOA Do Not Work for Some:

- Not trusting/doubtful of the process
- Contradicting beliefs
- Contradicting yourself/self-sabotage/thinking you're not deserving
- Mindset of lack
- Living in the past
- Thinking thoughts not in alignment with your desires
- Impatience
- Unhappiness

- Cannot focus because of old habits
- Too much resistance/not allowing the blessings and opportunities
- Too much effort or control/cannot let go or surrender to the Universe

Perhaps you may not be fully aware of the power within you because of your conditioned mind. You may only see yourself as small, and you may think you are not worthy to live your dream life because you never thought of yourself as the creator of your reality, but rather as just a victim of circumstance.

The worldviews have consumed you and you became fearful of stepping out of your comfort zone from knowing the unknown part of you. You are not just your physical body, but beyond it. Review your narrative about yourself now.

You can live and have the life you want. Be conscious of your power and start creating now!

REFLECTIONS

How do you look at yourself, a victim or a creator? Why?

How is your thinking pattern? How are you feeling most of the time?

What have you created in your life so far? Are you happy with your creation? How is it serving you?

What do you think of the Law of Attraction? How will it serve you?

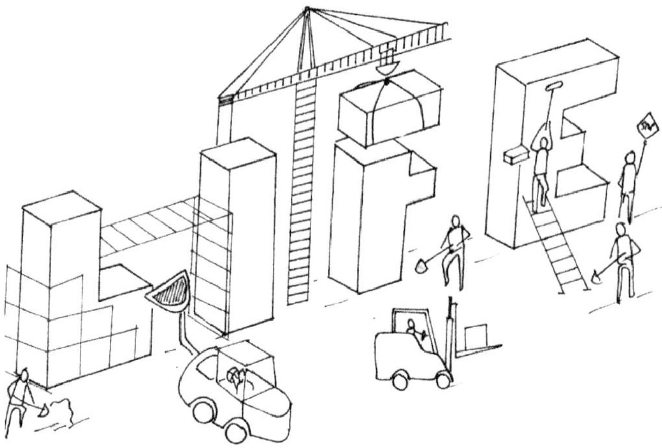
LIFE

CHAPTER THREE

REDESIGNING YOUR LIFE

Redesigning your life means taking, living, and experiencing your life to another level. It means bettering your "what ifs" and making them possible through the tools of creation and other resources inside you. It is a restart, creating a much better version or an update of your life.

If you have allowed yourself to receive the wisdom revealed to you in the previous chapters, you may now have remembered, realized, understood, and acknowledged the power within you based on your life experiences. You might have accepted that you are the creator of your reality and the experiencer of what you have created in your life. Based on your life now, you may already have clarity on the reasons you are stuck and challenged or felt free at other times.

When I recall my past creations through my experiences, I now understood that no one "must" make me happy, and no one is to blame for my failures and mistakes. I am the only one responsible for my life. I also recognized the choices I made through my decisions, which made me realize that **I always have choices, even when I chose not to make any decisions. That was a choice.** This choice is sometimes confused with being content and complacent.

As we are co-creating with each other, the current state of our world is the result of our creation through the physical manifestations of the quality of the thoughts we think about and focus our attention on. It is also the result of our beliefs...the collective consciousness. We can then create and redesign the world and life that we please and deserve with our power and choices. We start by redesigning our respective lives first, so we can share and contribute the wisdom we learned for the benefit and expansion of all.

Here are the basic keys you can consider in redesigning your life:

1. **Decisiveness** – the first key in redesigning your life. It means you have already considered and recognized the changes you should make in your life to improve and grow. You may be in pain or in any form of discomfort and confusion, but know that you can change your current state by recognizing the root cause of it.

Most of the time it's an error in thinking—meaning your choice and focus of thoughts are not in alignment with your inner being, the truth of who you are, and your desires. You are about peace, joy, and love. Pain arises when you are in contradiction with the truth. Because of this, the painful emotions are warning, teaching, and inspiring you to make a change.

Helpful Questions: **If there's one thing I want to change most in my life, what would that be? How will I change it? When will I change it?**

2. **Willingness** – as decisions can sometimes change and may feel like more of a sacrifice or an obligation, willingness is more committed. This is the second key in redesigning your life. It means you are opening your heart. Allowing your decision to make changes becomes more possible. It strengthens your decisions.

As you have recognized and made changes to fulfill your desires, you may sometimes feel uncomfortable when it comes to stepping out of your usual old habits of managing your challenges as you keep changing your decisions. Take your uncomfortable feelings of change as invitations for you to be more willing to commit to your goals. Let go of the excuses you hold on to. Know that you're gaining and winning when you're willing.

Helpful Questions: **Why am I still stuck when it comes to making changes and achieving my goals? What am I still holding on to? What is it I could not let go?**

3. **Openness** – this means you are welcoming and receiving the wisdom and lessons from your life experiences. You are open to see your life, the world, and humanity in a broader perspective. You see challenges and failures as opportunities, the world as the result of your creation, and other people as inspirations, not competitions.

You become more accepting and understanding of people and situations. Your decisiveness and willingness to change in redesigning your life will lead you to be more interested and have more zest in life. It is as if you are living for the first time. You are creating more space for your learning and expansion. Only when a heart is closed are fresh ideas opposed.

Helpful Questions: **What is it that challenges me the most to accept fresh ideas for my growth? Why am I not receptive? Why and what am I resisting? What beliefs have I accepted that do not work and serve me anymore?**

4. **Awareness** – this helps you to know that, as a creator, the world is abundant in everything that you need and require. What you need is always available for redesigning your life. As everyone is a physical extension of the Source energy, resources are not only limited to material things. Everyone and every situation are helpful sources of inspiration. They are your spiritual teachers, all rooting for you and telling you that all things are working out for you, no matter how situations may seem. When nothing is lacking, there's only more appreciating.

Helpful Question: **What is being shown to me that I could not see? What is the message I could not hear? What are these people, situations, and experiences teaching me?**

5. **Intentional** – this is an important key in your redesigning, as it focuses on your direction and

execution of your ideas in achieving your purpose and goals. With intention, we waste no amount of effort, ideas, or experiences. No one can be lost, as he is always guided by his innermost.

Helpful Questions: **Who and what would I like to become in redesigning my life? Where would I like to go? What would I like to happen? How would I like it to happen?**

Then there are helpful REMINDERS to reflect on as you redesign your life:

1. Know and believe that you are a creator, never a victim.
2. Go within, introspect. Self-inquire to know who you'd like to become. Meditate.
3. Recognize and observe what you need to work on and expand. Identify your stumbling blocks to move on to your desired direction. Is it fear, self-esteem issues, old beliefs, attachment from the past, anger, or guilt?
4. Know that you are responsible for your life and for discovering and harnessing your inherent power as a spiritual being.
5. Know your truth, your genuine nature. Express, live, and declare it. Say, "I am what I am, this is who I am, and this is my life and my creation. I

will keep creating more happiness, peace, joy, and love."

6. Know that you can reframe your beliefs. You can change your perception. You can change your narrative about your life and yourself. You are FREE.

7. Know that you are in a world of contrast. You can learn from the negative to turn it to positive. Appreciate how the learning journey serves you. Again, joy is being fulfilled in the journey.

8. Know that there are processes of emotions to go through that can make you feel stuck. They are teachers and reminders to empower yourself. Seek and focus on the lessons and wisdom, not on the suffering.

9. Know that there are many paths; you can start where you are or choose a fresh one. You always have choices.

10. Know that you are not alone but supported by the Universe/God/Divine Intelligence/Source who always has your back. Nothing is lacking.

A redesigned life is fresh, more purposeful, and in recognition of your power as a creator and in acknowledgment of your partnership with the Divine in co-creation. It is a life of vitality, zest, freedom, and living in appreciation and gratitude in all times. Consider equipping yourselves with these keys and reminders and start redesigning your lives to the lives you desire to have.

REFLECTIONS

What specific area/areas in your life need/s redesigning?

How can the basic keys help you in redesigning your life?

How will the reminders help and serve you? Which of the reminders you will need the most?

Are you ready to redesign your life? How are you going to start redesigning your life? Where are you going to start?

DESIGNER'S MANUAL
DESIGNER'S MANUA
BY ELSA MENDOZA

CHAPTER FOUR

DESIGN REFERENCES

There is something that motivates everyone. We do and say things prompted and inspired by something. We usually base this something on our influences, our programming, and the conditioning of our society. These come from the negative and positive state of minds, shaped by old beliefs that sometimes no longer work or are no longer applicable in the present times. They also limit us to be the grandest version of ourselves by not realizing our full potential restricted by our five senses.

We all desire a beautiful life, and we have different perceptions of what a beautiful life is. For some it could mean wealth, health, and adventure, but for others it means a simple life and being happy. How can we achieve a beautiful life? Is there any guide that we can refer to and rely on when seeking wisdom and truth in our journey to a beautiful life?

There are other resources we can refer to that we have not fully used and have forgotten or even taken for granted most of the time. This resource is from the power *within*...the non-physical part of us, which is always with us. This comes from the **power of our soul,** where our genuine power lies. It is limitless and beyond our five senses. It is the god in us that guides us every single second of every single day. We are never alone, as we are always guided and loved by our soul.

The Nonphysical Guides:

Our **Soul** is always whispering wisdom and guidance to us to get us through situations and people. This wisdom comes to us in impulses and hunches. Its agenda is evolution, harmony, unity, oneness, compassion, kindness, and love, a love that is always accepting. It's in reverence for life and it sees through everyone, everything, and every event. It is our **inner being and higher self,** always seeing us only through the eyes of love.

It understands the most difficult and recognizes the truth of one's intention and of every heart hiding in every word and action. It sees past the different masks and roles we portray to see the real reason behind the pain we experience. It also guides us to take other options to perceive our life's challenging situations for our spiritual growth. It helps us shift our victim perspective to a creative standpoint, telling us we can control how we respond to whatever difficulty is presented to us. It constantly reminds us of our power. It speaks through our intuition and feelings/emotions.

Intuition – is the voice of our soul. We know intuition as our gut feeling, our inner guidance. We all have this knowledge inside of us. We already know things subconsciously. Where did this knowledge come from? We are already equipped with it the moment we existed in this physical world. We knew how to breathe, feel, blink our eyes, move our hands and feet, and hear when we were children. Our internal organs know how to coordinate with each other miraculously and marvelously. Our wounds and scars knit and fade, and so does our pain. It's like running on autopilot.

As babies, we already know how to communicate with our parents through crying when we feel bad or need something. We smile and laugh, even if we did not fully understand what they said to us. We feel each other's energy and vibration, I suppose. We do not know how we know, but we just *knew,* all along.

When we feel something is "off" in situations we stumbled upon, our intuition helps us make the correct decisions. It serves like a compass, guiding us where to go or not to go. It inspires and nudges us to be in touch with people whom we haven't talked to for a while.

From time to time, we hear a voice of clarity or confirmation during our confusion, and suddenly we just knew the answers. We don't know how we knew, but we just did and it felt right. This feeling of rightness is in alignment with the truth of who we are.

The feelings of compassion and empathy for the hurt, kindness and love for the depressed, oppressed, abused, and battered—we all feel these sympathetic emotions without someone teaching us to do so. They just happen and come out of us naturally.

Sometimes, we remember someone and talk about this person and later that other person is already calling, texting, or emailing us. My cat George could not talk but communicated in unfamiliar meow tones, and I could understand what he meant and needed. When he looked at me, I could understand what he was trying to tell me.

The night my husband got into a car accident on the freeway, I had a strong yearning for him to come home. A few minutes afterward I got a text message from him saying he got into an accident but only had minor injuries, despite the immensity of the accident. We feel energies and vibrations we cannot fully explain in words, but then we can translate them accurately through our feelings.

There have been a few incidents in my life where my gut feeling was telling me to discontinue communication with certain people. This knowledge can serve as a valuable warning, too.

Feelings/Emotions – are the language of our soul. As mentioned in Chapter Two, they are also indicators of the quality of thoughts we think about. They are energies in motion.

Inexplicable things and events happen, happened, and are happening in our life. Sometimes there is no sure data to collect and no words could possibly describe a situation, but our feelings can explain them exactly. We're always translating and interpreting vibrations.

Just like thoughts and feelings, we do not see feelings and emotions until they manifest in the physical. Our feelings toward something, situations, and people send us signals. This tells us when to start, stop, wait, let go, or finish a project, relationship or situation.

I was once in a relationship with someone in the past where I wanted so badly for it to end. I literally prayed for the earth to open up and swallow me. It was an unpleasant experience. I just wanted to disappear. I was in agony. Then, one morning, I woke up and felt at peace. This peace gave me the strength and courage to do what I wanted to do, as if someone held my hand and guided me every step of the way to leave the relationship for good.

I learned from my experience that a person's sudden shift in emotions could change their consciousness and end their suffering. The person's painful thoughts shift to better thoughts as a start of a happier state, for example.

Try to recall where shifts happened in your life. Remember the peace, joy, and relief you felt after a predicament. We have translated these vibrations accurately because of their physical effects on us.

How do we know if the guidance received is from these non-physical sources? There is always **joy** in our thoughts, **clarity** and **truth** in our words, and **love** in our feelings. Only you can interpret this, as no one can think and feel for you. Therefore, advice from people is to serve as inspiration alone, because everyone has his own inner guidance for interpretation.

Guides and inspirations can also come from other sources that we already know, like music, poetry, movies, people, books, food, animals, nature, and even from situations we deemed impossible, bad, and unfair. Everything is being touched by the spirit of the Source. Everything is of God, remember?

When I say everything is of God, I am referring to the creation of contrast in this physical world, which is the world of polarity and relativity. Contrast is needed for the experience of the Infinite Creator's physical creations—otherwise, there's only a concept. A creator's job is to create, so he has to experience and know his creations, right? We are God's creations, and so we are co-creating with the Infinite Creator all the time.

You might ask, "And so are you saying God's job is only to create?"

Well, what do you think? Why was He/She/It/They called the Infinite Creator? Why do you think you are a creator, too? Why do you think you have heard some sources say that you are a god and that you are a child of God? Where do you think you come from? Why do you think the game of the Universe is creation? Why do you think nothing stays permanent? Why do you think evolution is the catalyst of change and the agenda of the soul? And why do you think life is a process of growth and that God is life and life is God? Observe the growth of everything, not only the physical but also the spiritual. I invite you to reflect on these questions.

A human being, for example, originated from the non-physical, spiritual world and part of the Divine consciousness, would only know he's human by experiencing his essence in this physical world through his senses and relationships.

Take me, for instance. I am called an author because of my experience in writing and publishing my book. Otherwise, how could I be called an author? I would only know the idea of being an author, not the experience.

Let's go back to our soul. As we grow older, we become insensitive to the nudges and whispers of our soul. Our material mind's powerful influence on us has perceived power as an external source only, usually in the form of wealth, title, rank, knowledge, and intelligence.

We have depended more on different influences for wisdom and direction and forgotten our inner guidance that is always available for us. We unconsciously (or consciously) accept and take the advice or truth of the majority as our own truth. This caused misalignment with who we truly are. We followed someone's truth and become deaf, blind, and numb. We were unable to hear, see, and feel our own truth.

The world and our lifestyles at present are the reflections and results of how we are all becoming disconnected from being in touch with our divine self—

the non-physical part of us. We are always on the go, on the run, hectic, busy, stressed, and burned out with crazy deadlines that we have allowed to control our lives. The balance of work and personal life affect our behavior, health, and relationships—and that balance is out of whack.

Our habits have contributed to the state we are in now. We have practiced and mastered beliefs that shaped our lives. It is best if we change our habits by changing our routine. If we have allowed ourselves to worry, we can also allow ourselves to be happy.

How can we go back to our truth and be sensitive to our inner guidance to help us redesign our life? We can start **by being still**, **pausing, meditating, introspecting, and being mindful**.

We can set aside a few minutes of our day to not do or think of anything but to take a breath and relax. We can do these sitting or lying in bed, before starting your work, during your breaks at work, in the car, or wherever may seem possible to do it. It helps you release whatever negative emotions you may have and improve your focus.

You can do it now. Wherever you are, if it's possible, pause and take a minute to close your eyes. Relax your head, eyes, ears, nose, tongue, lips, throat, neck, shoulders, arms, hands, fingers, chest, stomach, private parts, thighs, legs, feet and toes. Your body may feel heavy now and feel relaxed. Take a deep breath in, and hold it for a few seconds...and as you exhale and release, say a simple mantra: "I let go, thank you" and smile as you open your eyes. Do this twice more. Just so you know, I just did it with you. 😌

This is one of those pleasant habits you can add to your routine. You may start loving the experience and realize that you're doing it more often.

As you practice and focus on this breathing exercise or a quick meditation more often, you may notice yourself being more attuned with your inner being... more open to receiving and allowing yourself to be more in touch with your soul. You may feel at ease, relieved, and most of all, loved. Say yes to the Universe and it will do the rest. Feel its love embracing you once again. Breathe...

Be sensitive to your inner guides. Allow them to guide you. Use them. You are one with them and always connected to them. This is your truth, your nature as a spiritual being. They're always available and reliable, anytime, anywhere, all the time.

REFLECTIONS

Has there been a memorable experience in your life where you felt you're guided by the non-physical guides? What and how was it? What did you do?

What have you learned and realized in your me time and during your introspection?

Have you allowed yourself to refer to your non-physical guides? When and how is your experience?

"I write to the many,
but only a few will see, feel, and hear
The message that is clear for you, my dears
It takes the eyes of the Divine
to see beauty in everything
It takes the eyes of God to see beauty in everyone
It takes the eyes of the Source
to see beauty in every situation
It takes the eyes of love to experience beauty in all these
It takes faith and remembering that
you are a god expressed in human form
It takes courage to write this book,
believing everyone will see beauty in his
or her chosen path and journey called life
And say to themselves, 'yes, it is BEAUTIFUL, indeed!'"

Elsa Mendoza

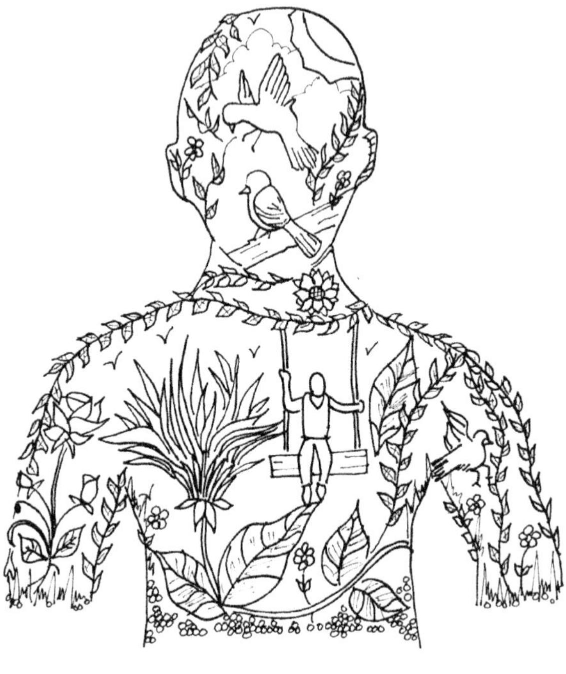

CHAPTER FIVE

THE BEAUTIFUL LIFE

What is a beautiful life? Is it a life full of beautiful people, things, and memories? How can one have a beautiful life?

Everyone desires to have a beautiful life. To fulfill such a desire can sometimes be a challenge, because of one's beliefs, priorities, and chosen lifestyle. Each individual has a different drive and interpretation of life, and this is influenced by his conditioned mind, which affects his outlook.

This physical world has strongly influenced us to deem a beautiful life through material things we have gained. We have unconsciously focused our attention too much on the physicality that we have forgotten our non-physical nature. We have become misaligned with the truth of our souls. It is about peace, joy, love, compassion, kindness, and bliss—which are also our original states.

But here we are, sometimes drowned in pain and suffering, causing more disease. The disease (or "dis-ease") I am referring to is not just about physical illnesses, but about internal and emotional struggles. These produce uncomfortable experiences as we go through them. They result from the quality of our beliefs/mindset.

As explained in the previous chapter, one has the power to create his own reality by remembering, acknowledging, believing in, and activating his power within. One can then free oneself from the bondages of limiting beliefs. As everyone is in partnership with the Source, it is possible to have a beautiful life despite challenging circumstances.

In this world of contrast, the positive cannot exist without the negative, so as happiness without sadness. Contrast helps us identify and understand our experiences, what we want and don't want, and who we truly are.

The common obstacles that stop us from experiencing the essence and beauty of Life:

- Resistance/not allowing ourselves to enjoy and grow
- Living in the past and future
- Living in Fear

- Living in someone's truth/beliefs
- Limiting/programmed/conditioned beliefs
- Separation beliefs
- Closed heart
- Ungratefulness
- Lack of appreciation
- Blame/passing the buck
- Ego/labels/identity

Since life is about creating experiences and everyone has his own unique one, I share with you the **how-tos** that have worked and served me. I believe they can serve you too, because I am your fellow human, a spiritual being experiencing life in the physical, just like you. I encourage you to ponder these:

A beautiful life is being experienced by:

1. **Deciding to live** – Many people just exist in their routine like a robot, accomplishing nothing—or only accomplishing the same thing again and again. Nothing happens or changes when there is no decision made. When you are willing and decided, the process called life takes place, and it shows endless possibilities to you.

You stop hoping and wishing. You *believe* again. Living is embracing life as it comes, not fighting against it.

2. **Showing up** – As I've said in the introduction, no one can live your life for you except you. Life is a gift. Receive this gift with gladness and appreciation. It is freedom to be, do, and have what you want.

3. **Believing and Trusting Life/Source/Universe** – Your faith backs your decisions. Nothing happens or materializes when you don't believe. As the saying goes, faith can move mountains. You live your life because you're assured by the love of the Divine Source. As you trust God, you also believe that the possibilities are endless. You become brave, independent, and fearless to seize each day and enjoy life.

4. **Connecting with the Source/Infinite Creator/ God** – It is good to always be in tune and connected with the Source of All. It will make you feel revitalized each day. The energy of the Source flows through you, but sometimes you can get lost and misaligned because of distractions from outside forces. Acknowledge and use the Source energy in states you are in. Ask, listen, and feel—it provides the wisdom you need. We find it everywhere, in everything, and in everyone. Even before you ask, an answer is already available.

5. **Being grateful** – A grateful heart sees beauty in everything. It witnesses miracles even in minor things. When you are thankful, life gives you more to be thankful for. It is about satisfaction and appreciation in many situations.

6. **Living your highest version** – You can live in excellence in all that you do and say by being your best without stressing or forcing yourself. This is your genuine nature. It is about giving without feeling obliged but out of love, as you are an embodiment of love. You represent not only yourself but the essence of the Perfect Creator. You were created magnificently, wonderfully, and perfectly, so express your creation for the benefit of humanity. This demonstration of excellence in your words and actions affects your community, and they will reap the harvest. You, leading by example, will inspire them to do the same, which then results in a beautiful cycle of living life to the fullest and giving our best to the entire world.

7. **Living in full awareness** – You are not just your physical body—your "earth suit." You, an indestructible spirit and physical extension of the Source, are invincible. When you are always in the seat of your soul, living without the influence of the ego but more on the spirit of God, nothing is being taken personally. There is a helpful question to remain in the experience of constantly living in full awareness: "How will your soul/higher self think and react if a hard

situation arises or if a challenging person is annoying you?" Remember, you are a god, too: a child of God, not of this world. You, like God, can love unconditionally.

8. **Living in the now** – The past is already gone, and when future comes, it will be in the present moment. The present keeps on showing up. Living in the past can bring about unnecessary suffering, as it invites regret. Living in the future makes you anxious. It makes you worry about and overthink something that hasn't transpired yet. The present is all there is. Focus on what is—appreciate and make the most of it.

9. **Living as if it's your first –** There is always an excitement in seeing, feeling, witnessing, learning, and experiencing things, situations, places, and people for the first time. Live each day in this attitude and witness the joy and change it brings.

10. **Living as if it's your last –** Live your life to the fullest. Do not waste your time in pointless activities such as being nosy, whining, gossiping, judging, and engaging in petty quarrels. Make the most out of everything. Always be growing, happy, and loving. It helps you savor and appreciate each moment of your life.

11. **Thinking in alignment with who you truly are** – When living in alignment with who you truly

are—and remember, you are limitless, abundant, knowing, and loving—you think and act like the Divine and like the masters who have walked on this earth: living in power and in love.

12. **Knowing your intention** – It is beneficial to know how to get and achieve your purpose by the quality of your intentions. Define your purpose and your reason and then know how to get there by your actions and intentions. When there is intention there is direction.

13. **Staying inspired and not expired** – When life isn't always up and cheery, you may sometimes feel worn and burned out. Know that everything and everyone is a source of inspiration. You can never run out of inspiration. The Universe's game is an endless joyful creation and expansion. Even before our need arises, the provisions are already available. Look, see, and feel your way through. Life is always working for you. The emotions you feel, the challenging people you meet, and the tough situations you experience are your teachers. You're always supported and guided. Turn your life around to the life you so deserve.

14. **Being curious** – As a creative being, learning and discovering are endless. Never tire from inquiring. This invites more growth. The more you grow, the more the Universe grows and expands, too. This is how you evolve. Curiosity

is living each day in wonderment as if it's your first. It is a great attitude as it causes you to probe, ask, and learn more from your inner guidance.

15. **Learning something new** – When you learn, you discover more of who you are and what you have. You can do something you have not done before. Always be a student full of curiosity. Enroll yourself in classes that interest you and engage in activities that you have not done before. There is always something new to your senses each day, when you are open to learn. You can involve yourself in healthy discussions for your spiritual growth. As Eleanor Roosevelt said, "Great minds discuss ideas; average minds discuss events; small minds discuss people."

16. **Living on purpose** – It is living your passion and creation. It gives you zest and a sense of yourself and of life itself, as your purpose is to create who you'd like to be and declare it in every moment.

17. **Opening your heart** – It is seeing through people, things, events, and situations only by observation and without judgment. It is through openness that we develop more understanding. We find their essence, beauty, lessons, and wisdom.

18. **Loving yourself** – Taking good care of yourself spiritually, mentally, emotionally, and physically helps you in living life to the fullest. By taking care of your needs first, you can provide more for others. Let people know about the value of your personal space. You are teaching people how to treat you. You can love others when you have love for yourself without feeling obliged, suffering, or sacrificing.

19. **Unleashing and activating your power within** – Know that the Infinite Creator made you in magnificence and perfection. You are a co-creator. Go forth and create wondrous things through the power within you and the tools of creation you're equipped with. You are about boldness, not timidity. Create in love and out of love for the benefit of all. Use your gifts and talents to inspire and guide everyone you have attracted in your life. As you expand, the Universe also expands through your evolution. Your contribution is vital.

20. **Speaking Life** – Words are energy. Words are also the second level of the creation process. These are thoughts expressed. What you say or declare about yourself and your situation matters, because there's power in words that can either make or break you—they can even make or break a nation. Listen to confident people talk, motivational speakers and positive people. Notice how you feel afterward. You feel empowered and want to listen and hang out

more with them, right? You can start speaking words that promote encouragement, uplift-ment, and love.

21. **Doing the things you love and enjoy** – There is nothing more satisfying than doing what you love. When you love what you do, you excel more. You are more inspired. You bring outstanding results. You also serve others more effortlessly, not expecting anything in return. Find out what you want and love most, and just do it. It could be small for you, but remember: the small things make up the enormous things.

22. **Minding your own business** – You grow and learn more about yourself when you focus only on your life. Your life is about *you,* not about others. That may sound selfish, but it is not. How can you live for others if your life is in shambles? You cannot give and share what you do not have. You cannot teach what you do not know. I am referring to you living your own life and being liable to it. Focus on changing your own life instead of other people's lives. As you change your life, you affect society. You affect our world.

23. **Being like YOU, not like him/her/them** – Every person is unique in personality and choices. Embrace your uniqueness—your weirdness, if you will. Enjoy being you, the extraordinary and original you. Know your truth and live with it.

Those who love you will love you more with your authenticity.

24. **Being mindful of the beliefs, conditioning, and influences of your society** – The collective consciousness can sometimes cause you to forget your true nature or create confusion therein. You have a wealth of wisdom that only you can decipher. You can decide what beliefs to take in and which beliefs will serve and work for you. Listen to your intuition more. Your gut feeling/intuition is your soul/God talking to you. Let it be your guide.

25. **Willingness to receive and accept** – When you give more, you get more. Sometimes you don't get what you want, as you forget that you are also deserving of what you give out. It's the cycle of abundance, the Law of Sowing and Reaping, or the Law of Compensation. Give out and receive in. Don't block the flow of your blessings.

26. **Knowing your tribe** – Everyone and everything is a source of inspiration, be it negative or positive. You can surround yourself with sources of love and beauty, as well as those who are in the same goal as you. Many are acquaintances, but few are your friends. Be mindful of your time, especially with whom, what, and where you spend it. It is very much okay to be selective of who and what you expose yourself to. This is about protecting

your energy. As you become more “you,” you will begin to attract those with the same vibration/energy/frame of mind as yours.

27. **Letting go of the negative resources –** Let go of those who do not bring out the best in you. Cease wasting your energy and time on negativities. Focus on feeling good. Attract the people, situations and environments you would like to be with and in.

28. **Allowing, more than resisting –** There is a natural order and timing. Be patient—do not force or pressure yourself or situations. Allow things to happen as they will. It is about trusting and witnessing how the Universe gathers the cooperative elements and conspires to bring exactly what you desire. One can use judgment, when there is an obvious danger, to protect oneself. This can sometimes be necessary, despite how impossible it is for one’s evolution.

29. **Blessing all –** When you look through the eyes of the Source, you have knowledge that all events and occurrences are happening in its fashion and working for your benefit, growth, and evolution. You understand that the Source of all is in control no matter what. Bless, do not curse. Keep in mind that what you give out comes back to you. Like energy attracts like energy.

30. **Forgiving** – It is about giving love and freeing yourself from guilt. You're loved and never judged. Only your thoughts and the negative stories you add to them are judgmental. It is also freedom from a mindset of separation from God and all. Everyone is a part of the Divine consciousness. Release yourself from this kind of mindset and move on.

31. **Expecting nothing** – The higher your expectation, the higher your frustration. You hurt so much because you expect too much. Life is freedom. Free yourself from attachment and the result of what you have done. Start living and noticing a happier life. As William Shakespeare said, "Expectation is the root cause of all heartaches."

32. **Changing your narrative** – Have no fear of changing your beliefs about yourself, people, life, and even about the God of your own beliefs. Nothing and no one remains unchanged. You are continuously evolving from your experiences. These experiences are teachers for your expansion. Keep growing and inquiring. Disregard beliefs that promote further separation from the Source of all and those that no longer serve you and welcome the new.

33. **Living in a winner's mindset** – You are never a victim. People and situations that you think are

against you are teachers for your growth. When you fix your thinking, life fixes itself.

34. **Living in humility** – Being humble is not about arrogance and needing attention. It is living without being attached to the ego's whims: superiority, competition, and separation. It is being mostly driven by **love**. It is also having an attitude and a heart of service to others. As C.S. Lewis said, "Humility is not thinking less of yourself. It's thinking of yourself less."

35. **Living in simplicity** – Simple living is not about having fewer things but about your relationship with these things. It is about keeping only the essentials needed to live a life worth living, despite what the world is demanding. It is letting go of things and people that do not serve you, such as complicated relationships, hard people, and difficult situations. It is living without attachments, especially to the ego.

36. **Communing with nature** – Nature has healing magic for all of us. Its sounds, smells, feelings, and presence bring ease and peace. Spend more time in it. People find not only healing but a lot of inspiration in nature. Appreciate its beauty made for us. It's an expression of love for love. It is God communing with you.

37. **Taking responsibility** – Since you are the only one who can live your life, you are accountable for it. It is about speaking your truth, living your

truth, and owning your truth. By owning this, you empower yourself to alter it again according to your liking as you grow. It is also knowing that your life is the result of your own thinking and doing, therefore not blaming someone else for its outcome.

38. **Living your own experience** – Life is most beautiful when you enjoy your own experience based on your own realization, discovery, and remembrance—your very own truth. Since the millennia, humanity has been heeding and living the truth based on sources and beliefs that have tainted, dampened, deceived, and created more damage. One needs to find one's genuine nature: oneness with the Divine Source of All. Live to the fullest by listening to that small voice within you. There is nothing more liberating and joyful than living your own truth.

39. **Not being moved by circumstances** – Your faith keeps you focused and centered at the seat of the soul, where you remain in awareness that all things are working out for your benefit regardless of how circumstances may seem.

I believe that all of us have undergone a crisis in our lives we thought we would not survive. Not only did we survive, but we thrived and became more appreciative of life and its lessons afterward. We transformed, discovered more of our powers, and understood more of ourselves after each crisis. These crises must take place for us to experience ease, as well as to celebrate and appreciate the beauty of life. Life then becomes more interesting, meaningful, and most of all, beautiful. However, for some, life is being interpreted, perceived, and lived in unique ways. It depends on one's experience and realizations. The goodness about life is that it is consistent with being one with you, and it's always happening in the present moment.

Living the Beautiful Life gives you an opportunity to:

1. **Experience God/Creator** – Regardless of whether you're a believer of God, you can agree that there is a mysterious force/energy/source that embraces us all together. This energy flows through each one of us. Humanity has labeled this energy with many names: Source, Force, Energy, God, Infinite Creator, Supreme Being, Divine Entity, and Universe, to name a few. Wherever you go and whatever you do, this force is with you. You exist as a human being to experience the creation of the Infinite One. There's no beginning and end where the Creator is not present. It is limitless and eternal. From nothingness to formlessness, the Source is also in there. Realize it. To understand it, you will be out of your mind to grasp it, but one thing is for sure: you just know and sense it.

2. **Experience its beauty** – Life is a process complicated to explain. It's possible to get lost in bewilderment when figuring it out. Some of our experiences can be unpleasant and uncomfortable at first, but the total experience is beautiful. The twists and turns are the cooperative components needed for our growth, and they can lead us to where, what, and who we're supposed to be. Our challenges can take us for a ride and give us lessons and wisdom. When we create our reality, life elevates and gravitates. The results are always beneficial for our expansion. Realize its order and provisions.

3. **Experience abundance** – Before humanity ever existed, the essentials needed for survival were already available. The early human settlers on this earth survived and thrived with the basic provisions. Nothing is lacking. It is always enough. Only our thoughts of scarcity and actions of greed and selfishness defy these. Life is consistently giving us and other sentient beings what we need every single moment of each day. The animal kingdom's daily survival is the best example and inspiration for us.

4. **Experience peace** – The process called life is peaceful. Notice the growth of plants and trees, the birth of other sentient beings. It happens without disturbing the order of things but brings us tranquility and healing as we commune with nature. As we are one with life,

life gives us chances to realize and remember that we are also the embodiment of peace.

5. **Experience joy –** It is one of our true essences. We were born with it, from it, and we are the embodiment of it in the flesh, like peace and love.

6. **Experience love –** With the absence of life and God, we cannot experience love, as they are all one. Love is the essence of living and vice versa. It is the driving force of the entirety of life.

7. **Build relationships –** One joy of living is that we can share and show our love through our relationships. It is the sharing of each other's completeness with each other. It is through relationships that we find the depths and beauty of our souls.

8. **Share your gifts and talents –** As we are love in the flesh, we express more of it with our creativity. We excel in our chosen field of expertise that we can contribute to the betterment of the world, solve problems, heal sickness, bring order and peace in chaos, and teach the confused, to name a few.

9. **Help and serve people –** One cannot live or serve without love, as love *is* giving and communing with each other.

10. **Inspire and empower –** We learn that we can teach and we have the strength to empower

each other. Whatever we gain, we give. What we plant, we reap. This is a natural and a continuous cycle of life.

11. **Experience oneness –** As you live this life, you realize that we're all woven together. We're connected. We all have love in our hearts to provide compassion, kindness, healing, encouragement, and empowerment in times of need, regardless of the separation beliefs we have all created. We are one community serving one another.

12. **Experience who you truly are –** Every moment is a moment of remembering your genuine nature. Every life experience gives you the opportunity to discover your capabilities, gifts, and talents. Life helps you realize how you handle situations and celebrations. It helps you know your strengths and weaknesses.

13. **Experience the importance of your role –** As you are part of the whole, a co-creator of God, and a member of humanity, you are a contributor to the world. Your contributions make up this world. You may not be an inventor, manager, president, or chairman, but a company exists not only with these positions. You always have something to offer, or a gift to give someone. Your understanding, listening heart, humor, compassion, and even your smile can make a vast difference to someone in need. Everyone is special.

14. **Express your creativity –** There is a vast amount of creative expressions in this world through art, technology, and innovation that have furthered the development and progress of our world since the earliest times. We should be in awe and thankful for the possibilities of our ideas materializing.

15. **Do what you love** – Nobody's stuck in doing what he/she despises. We hear stories about people who found their passion through many trials. There are many inspiring and courageous people who took a leap of faith and left their lucrative careers to do what they truly love. They did it by taking heed of that voice inside them and *decided*. You always have a choice in this life: to change your career path, change its direction, and find that meaningful career, passion, or hobby that makes your heart sing. Life is freedom.

16. **Experience your power** – When we are in our lowest moments, we discover our powerful self. It helps us flourish. Life lets us remember our power, and then own and embrace it.

17. **Create a new you** – Change is the only permanent thing in this life. The beauty of it is that we get better not because we're awful, but we remember who we truly are and keep growing. We never stop evolving. This world of contrast motivates us so as we identify what we want and what we don't want.

18. **Learn from it** – Difficulties and challenges happen so we can experience the lessons and extract the wisdom out of them to start living a more meaningful life.

19. **Flourish** – Our experiences are available for our growth. When we get knocked down, we always get up. Some may take time, but we always thrive, survive, and remain alive despite circumstances.

20. **Make choices** – We are all free to know what works and serves us from every situation presented to us.

21. **Change** – This makes life more interesting. Nothing stays permanent except change. It must happen for creation to start and for the Universe to expand.

22. **Correct your mistakes** – Life provides us chances to start from scratch and better our approach and execution of our beliefs, systems, rules, and regulations. It is forgiving.

23. **Rectify problems** – Life always gives us a choice to make things easier or harder for ourselves.

24. **Know that life only exists in the present moment** – Life is not in our past nor in our future; it is always happening in the now. It reminds us to relax and enjoy the moment of now.

25. **Enjoy it** – Every opportunity is giving us a chance and a choice on what to do with it. It invites and asks what you will do next. As life is always with you and in you, it is generously gifting you the time to revel in it.

26. **Live it** – We come and live in the physical world to experience humanity and life. Some people only have a brief time to live their lives. They don't waste any second of it. They show up. You can consider asking yourself if you are fully living or just existing.

27. **Appreciate it** – How many times have you survived pain and suffering, then thrived afterward? The rhythm of life makes you thankful to be alive. It helps you realize that, no matter what, you come out whole in the end, out of every challenge you face. It lets you appreciate the experience.

28. **Accept it** – Nothing is more satisfying than living in non-resistance. You just go with the flow, trusting the Universe/God has your back in all circumstances.

29. **Understand it** – There is beauty in the mystery of life, most especially the beauty of the Infinite Creator who created it. Everyone has a unique interpretation, and every time, there is a fresh revelation of what life is. Focus on what it has provided and done for you and find out what it tells you. Observe.

30. **Put meaning in it –** We can define life by our experiences. We can find meaning even in the smallest of things. We are free to label it based on our awareness of it.

31. **Experience contrast** – This helps us identify what we want and do not want. It causes us to ask, investigate, and weigh our choices in life as we create our reality or our life experience.

32. **Experience the tides of it –** The rhythm of life helps us dance to its tempo and realize its beautiful essence, as we always become powerful creators and not victims. It refines, purifies, and renews. It helps us remember our genuine nature: love.

Life is interestingly beautiful! It is eternal. From its formlessness, nothingness, consciousness, and the non-physical to the creation of the physical world, it is wonderful to experience what the Infinite Creator has created through us.

In this physical world of contrast, the ego exists and plays its role. When you observe the ego, its role is really to help us remember who we are through our realizations from its actual intention, which makes us forget our genuine nature as spiritual beings, and keeps us from our spiritual growth. The yin and yang, the negative and positive, are vital. One cannot realize and experience something in the other's absence. One would not know good without knowing the bad, long without the short, and light without the dark—to name a few.

Beliefs—otherwise known as the creations of men—caused us to forget who we truly are, our non-physical, spiritual part of us. We have come up with labels and believed that we are sinners and imperfect beings at birth, despite our origins from a perfect and Infinite Creator.

If one can see through it all, there is no right, wrong, or judgment in the eyes of the Source. The gift of freewill helps us decide and choose. It is neither right nor wrong; it is what serves your purpose, unless you perceived or deemed it right or wrong. Love only abounds. Only humans are judgmental of themselves, because they are influenced by the separation beliefs. These judgments have limited us to be the grandest versions of ourselves. We've come up with dogmas supporting these.

We only become close to imperfection in the process of creation, as it is a never-ending trial and error, learning and unlearning, realizing, discovering, remembering who we truly are, and expressing and declaring it until we're ready for another cycle of creation again. There's perfection in imperfection through the process of creation, if one can realize.

It is through us that the Infinite Creator can experience everything. Therefore, who and what the Infinite Creator is, is who and what we are. We're made from His/Her/Their image and likeness. This image is not referring to the physical form, but to its essence. We are the extension of the Source. We are all interconnected as one. What you do unto others, you do unto yourself. How you see others reflects you, and how you react to others is an awareness of yourself. There are really no others, if you think about it—just unique versions of ourselves. The condition of the earth reflects what and who we have become.

The rise of the different beliefs and teachings that are fear-based causes confusion and separation. There are so many egotistic influences contributing to further separation, pain, and suffering. It is difficult to remember our true selves, our inherent power. It is even more difficult to love ourselves.

We think we are not worthy. We have become unconscious. However, this pain and suffering that we experience always leads us to a shift of consciousness that we may wake up and remember who we truly are and recognize our power. This is how we can get back to our state of oneness, back in union with Divine Source.

Life is what we make it. Our purpose is to create, grow, and expand, and we will do this having been fueled by our desires, which are also the Soul's/God's desire, as we are one with the Source. Everything works for our benefit, yet there are times we get stuck. This is caused by the effect of our negative emotions and the victim mindset.

You may look at life and our world as a game of giving and receiving, where what you give out, you will receive, as evidenced by the Law of Cause and Effect—similar to the Law of Attraction.

The abounding love and the promise of the Infinite Creator is for us to receive what we asked for, provided that we ask. Enlightened teachers, like other bringers of light, have set examples of what a human being's power is: to create through the usage of the conscious and subconscious minds with thoughts, words, actions, and faith. They exhibited power, a life lived in love, compassion, and kindness, and of faith, that can inspire and empower us to do and live by these.

It's time to create alternative systems inspired by Divine Intelligence, looking through everyone. We do this not just as physical beings but as energies, souls, and spiritual beings based on inclusion, oneness, and love. If we have all allowed hatred to rule our hearts, we can also allow love to rule our body, mind, and spirit.

We can change our narratives about these now. We can change how we have viewed and allowed ourselves to believe who we are. We can start redesigning our lives and creating from within a life worth living.

REFLECTION

What is a beautiful life for you? How would you like to experience its beauty?

Describe how your life is at present?

What is the current state of your life? How would you like to spend the rest of it?

AUTHOR'S NOTE

I wrote this book to ask humanity one of life's big questions: "What are you doing with your life?"

In my last two books, *Wake Up Humanity* and *Come Back to Love*, I asked the questions: "What kind of source are you?" and "What are you doing with yourself?" I want to say this book completes those questions I wanted to ask you. This might be the last stand-alone question as you continue delving deeper within yourselves.

I write books to share my life story and the wisdom gained from my spiritual journeys. I want to share lessons learned from my life experience and from the teachings of other inspiring people. It is about an endless introspection, peeling layers and layers from decades of programming, beliefs, and influences that made me forget the real me. I have changed and continue to change the narrative I allowed myself to believe from the said programming, and I love who I have become and am still becoming. I keep discovering, remembering, and being reminded of the truth of who I am in my moments of reflection, meditation, challenges, and choices I face, relationships I am in, and with my emotional journey.

I invite you, dear reader, to inquire within, as the answers you seek are just within you, waiting for you to discover them. There is a well and wealth of wisdom in every individual, as everyone is an extension of the Source. As you find these answers, you'd be very much guided to redesign your life as they align with your higher self.

When I was just gathering, chasing, and grasping thoughts of inspiration for this book, it inspired me to compare life to a salad. My husband found it funny, and asked me, "Why a salad?" My answer was simple: life is like a salad in a bowl—the bowl represents the Universe, where we're all held together. Every ingredient represents each one of our gifts, giving the "salad" its unique taste and flavor. Mixing all the ingredients is the creation process of our reality, our life experiences. Enjoying your "salad" represents living your beautiful life in this world.

As I read, study, listen, reflect, think, and write, I grow as a person and as an author. In the process of my writing journey, I observe the whims of my ego in war with my actual intention. I am thankful for the number of naps I took. I am grateful for the time I spent petting my cat George and the snacks I had on my breaks so I could gain my momentum and get back at it again.

I ask myself these questions just before I write: How will truth say it? How will peace say it? How will love write it?

It's important for me to be in alignment with my experiences about my truth, clarity, peace, joy, and love when I write—most especially without imposing. I'm also thankful for the guidance of the Divine Intelligence, for all the wisdom you can find in this book, and for using me as an instrument. I recognize as my perceptions expand, I develop a deeper understanding of life, the world, its people, and the Source.

Until next time...

Elsa Mendoza

LIFE

A game and a cycle you are
Up and down every hour
The belief is you are short
I say only if you support
In free will I create my reality
I ask if there is a guarantee
As I create
You gravitate and elevate
You let me see what I'd like to see
That there is only one permanency
Change is always present in me
It is what we make it they say
I believe in the hearsay
You are not to be wasted, I pray
But to be appreciated always

By: Elsa Mendoza From the book:
Wake Up Humanity Poems About You and Me

REQUEST

If you have enjoyed my book, it would be greatly appreciated if you left a review so others can receive the same benefits you have. Your review will help me see what is and isn't working so I can better serve you and other readers even more.

ACKNOWLEDGEMENTS

I am eternally thankful to our Divine Intelligence for inspiring me to write this book.

To you, beautiful soul, reader, supporter, and believer of my works, I am in gratitude to you for purchasing my books. I am so inspired to write more.

To my loving and supportive husband, for the illustrations of the book and for always challenging me to write at my best and to take this book to another level.

am grateful for the services and works of my beautiful editor, Qat Wanders of Wandering Words Media/ www.qatwanders.com, my wonderful formatter, Jen Henderson of Wildwords Formatting Services/ www.wildwordsformatting.com and an outstanding book cover designer, Les, who have all done excellent jobs in making this book possible. Thank you, too, to my talented makeup artist and photographer, Ferdie Washington for always making me look and feel beautiful in my profile photo.

To my incredible launch team, I am inspired by each one of you, and I am always touched by your support, a million thanks again and again.

To SPS, the Self-Publishing School that taught me to become a self-published author. I am in gratitude to all the staff.

Thank you all so very much from my heart and soul.

ABOUT THE AUTHOR

Elsa Mendoza is a Certified Community Life Coach who has a passion for uplifting, empowering, encouraging, motivating, inspiring, and helping others to find their passion in life. She helps people identify their strengths and potential, as well as to change their mindset and old paradigms for a better life and relationship to themselves and to others. Her motivation in doing so is her endurance from living with a harsh family environment during her childhood until her early twenties and overcoming a rare disease that almost took her life.

She believes in the power of the human mind, its thoughts, and the laws of the Universe. She is always curious, a thinker and a seeker. She is confident in the power of humanity and the possibility of a much better world where oneness exists.

Elsa is well traveled, has lived in different countries, and has interacted with several nationalities. She has been exposed to different lifestyles, cultures, and religions, and has seen what humanity has to offer—thus her inspirations for writing this book.

She holds a Masters of Science degree in International Business at California International University where she has helped small companies thrive in operations and sales. In her free time, she volunteers at Long Beach Rescue Mission. She loves reading, watching movies, plays, and concerts, playing with her cat George, and traveling with her husband.

Also by Elsa Mendoza

YOU CAN QUOTE ME ON THIS

Words to Empower You
and Awaken Your Consciousness
https://www.amazon.com/dp/B0721HWK3V

WAKE UP HUMANITY

Poems About You and Me
https://www.amazon.com/gp/product/B07DK5GF1I

COME BACK TO LOVE

Understandings and Reflections on Self-Love

https://www.amazon.com/gp/product/B07SSH5YJW/

CONNECT WITH THE AUTHOR

Email: elsa@changecreateevolve.com

Follow her on:

https://www.facebook.com/Change.Create.Evolve/

http://changecreateevolve.com

https://www.instagram.com/your_coach_elsa/

https://twitter.com/Lsavm

https://www.amazon.com/Elsa-Mendoza/e/B071K4XBYQ

https://www.goodreads.com/author/show/16945935.Elsa_Mendoza

https://partners.bookbub.com/authors/4402533/edit

https://www.pinterest.com/elsav_mendoza/boards/

REFERENCES

BOOKS:

Wake Up Humanity Poems About You and Me by Elsa Mendoza

Come Back to Love Understandings and Reflections on Self-Love by Elsa Mendoza

The Law of Attraction The Basics of the Teachings of Abraham by Esther and Jerry Hicks

If Life is a Game, These are The Rules Ten Rules for Being Human by Cherie Carter Scott, Ph.D.

The Seat of The Soul: 25th Anniversary Edition with a Study Guide by Gary Zukav

The Astonishing Power of Our Emotions Let Your Feelings Be Your Guide by Esther and Jerry Hicks

eBooks

Wallace D. Wattles – New Thought: HOW TO GET WHAT YOU WANT, THE SCIENCE OF GETTING RICH, THE SCIENCE OF BEING WELL, THE SCIENCE OF BEING GREAT https://www.amazon.com/Wallace-D-Wattles-Thought-SCIENCE-ebook/dp/B086N595RV

The Prentice Collection https://www.amazon.com/Prentice-Mulford-Collection-ebook/dp/B007QYD8P2

ONLINE

Universe definition https://www.collinsdictionary.com/dictionary/english/universe

What Buddha Knew About the Law Of Attraction https://livealifeyoulove.com/buddha-knew-law-of-attraction/

100 Bible Verses on Thoughts and The Mind https://www.openbible.info/topics/thoughts_and_the_mind

25 Bible Quotes that Tie in with the Teachings of the Law of Attraction by Alan Young https://subconsciousservant.com/law-of-attraction-bible-quotes/

Your Intuition & Inner Guidance – Explained by Abraham Hicks by Real Tarot Reading
https://youtu.be/CYaMw-gLBV0

Abraham Hicks – What is Intuition? By Good Life
https://youtu.be/DrOkK09uk_U

Who Discovered the Law of Attraction: Uncovering the Truth by Howard Poole
https://manifestwithease.com/who-discovered-law-of-attraction/

What's the Difference Between a Feeling and an Emotion? by Neel Burton M.D.
https://www.psychologytoday.com/us/blog/hide-and-seek/201412/whats-the-difference-between-feeling-and-emotion

Three Differences between Emotions and Feelings
https://exploringyourmind.com/three-differences-emotions-and-feelings/

Printed in Great Britain
by Amazon

49647056R00078